Rookie Read-About® Science

Vegetables, Vegetables!

By Fay Robinson

Consultants
Robert L. Hillerich, Professo
Bowling Green State University, Bo
Consultant, Pinellas County Sc

Lynne Kepler, Educational

CHILDRENS

CHICA

Design by Beth Herman Design Associates
Photo Research by Feldman & Associates, Inc.

Library of Congress Cataloging-in-Publication Data

Robinson, Fay.
    Vegetables, vegetables! / by Fay Robinson.
      p. cm. – (Rookie read-about science)
    ISBN 0-516-06030-9
    1. Pumpkin–Juvenile literature. 2. Vegetables–Juvenile literature.
[1. Pumpkin.] I. Title. II. Series.
SB347.R63   1994
635'.62-dc20   94-14075
                                      CIP
                                      AC

Do you like the
smell and taste of
pumpkin pie . . .

the taste and feel of a
sweet, crunchy carrot . . .

the colorful sight of bright,
ripe peppers?

These foods are all vegetables.
Vegetables come from parts of
certain plants.

Some vegetables, like lettuce, are the leaves of a plant.

Others, like radishes, are
the roots of a plant.

Peas and lima beans
are a plant's seeds.

Some vegetables, like onions, are bulbs.

When you eat broccoli or cauliflower, you are eating a plant's flowers.

Vegetables with seeds are a plant's fruit.

To a scientist, a fruit is the part of a plant that covers the seeds. So vegetables with seeds inside, like tomatoes,

13

14

cucumbers, and pumpkins, are actually fruits.

But we usually call them vegetables. They aren't sweet, like most fruits we know.

People eat vegetables in many ways. Raw vegetables can be cut up to make a salad . . .

or to eat as snacks.

Vegetables can be cooked alone . . .

or cooked with other things to make soups, stews, and even breads.

Carrot bread makes a great, healthy snack.

Farmers grow vegetables in most parts of the world.

Many people grow their own vegetables in gardens.

It's fun to plant the seeds . . .

give them plenty of water . . .

and watch them grow.

Vegetables are good for you. They have lots of important vitamins, minerals, and fiber.

If you have a chance to help prepare them, vegetables taste especially delicious.

To make a great salad,
have a grown-up help
you cut up
some lettuce,
a carrot,
a tomato,
a cucumber,
and a green pepper.

Put on your favorite salad dressing or eat it plain.

Yum!

Words You Know

vegetables

garden

salad

pumpkins

carrot   peppers   lettuce

radishes   peas   cucumbers

broccoli   cauliflower   tomatoes

31

Index

breads, 18, 19
broccoli, 11, 31
bulbs, 10
carrot, 4, 26, 31
carrot bread, 19
cauliflower, 11, 31
cucumbers, 15, 26, 31
farmers, 20
fiber, 25
gardens, 21, 30
green pepper, 26
lettuce, 7, 26, 31
lima beans, 9
minerals, 25
onions, 10
peas, 9, 31
peppers, 5, 26, 31
plants, 6
 plant's flowers, 11
 plant's fruit, 12, 15
plant's leaves, 7
plant's roots, 8
plant's seeds, 9
pumpkin pie, 3
pumpkins, 15, 30
radishes, 8, 31
raw vegetables, 16
roots of a plant, 8
salad, 16, 26, 30
salad dressing, 28
seeds, 12
 planting seeds,22
 watering seeds, 23
snacks, 17, 19
soups, 18
stews, 18
tomatoes, 12, 26, 31
vegetables, 6, 10, 12, 15, 16, 18,
 20, 21, 25, 30
vitamins, 25

About the Author

Fay Robinson is an early childhood specialist who lives and works in the Chicago area. She received a bachelor's degree in Child Study from Tufts University and a master's degree in Education from Northwestern University. She has taught preschool and elementary children and is the author of several picture books.

Photo Credits

PhotoEdit – ©David Young-Wolff, 4, 11, 17, 19, 21, 22, 30 (top right), 31 (top left and bottom center); ©Michael Newman, 18 (top), 29; ©Stephen McBrady, 23; ©Elizabeth Zuckerman, 24; ©Myrleen Ferguson, 27

SuperStock International, Inc. – 10; ©Micheal Rutherford, Cover; ©Rivera Collection, 5, 9, 16, 30 (bottom left), 31 (top center and center center); ©David Forbert, 6, 30 (top left); ©George Glod, 8, 31 (center left); ©Herb Levart, 13, 31 (bottom right); ©David Spindell, 14, 31 (center right)

Unicorn Stock Photos – ©Martha McBride, 3, 30 (bottom right); ©Jim Hays, 7, 31 (top right); ©Fred D. Jordan, 18 (bottom); ©Jim Shippee, 31 (bottom left)

Valan – ©Christine Osborne, 20

COVER: Vegetables